All I Want for Christmas Is . . .

Marry Christmas

All I Want for Christmas Is...

LETTERS FROM SANTA'S MAILBAG

Compiled by

Carl Anderson, Ph.D.

and

Jim Walker Jr.

Health Communications, Inc.
Deerfield Beach, Florida

www.hci-online.com

Library of Congress Cataloging-in-Publication Data

All I want for Christmas is— : letters from Santa's mailbag / compiled
   by Carl Anderson and Jim Walker, Jr.
      p. cm.
    ISBN 1-55874-636-6 (trade paper)
    1. Santa Claus. 2. Children's writings. I. Anderson, Carl.
   II. Walker, Jim.
GT4985.A43 1998
394.2663—dc21   98-29010
                                                      CIP

©1998 Carl Anderson and Jim Walker Jr.
ISBN 1-55874-636-6

Publisher: Health Communications, Inc.
             3201 S.W. 15th Street
             Deerfield Beach, FL 33442-8190

Cover design by Larissa Hise.

We dedicate this book to everyone who dreams of sleigh bells in the sky, reindeer on the roof, something special in their stocking, and warmth in the hearts of all people.

We also dedicate this book to the volunteers who graciously give of themselves each year in the spirit of Santa Claus to make a child's world a little brighter and full of hope and love.

Contents

Acknowledgments

I t is well-known that even Santa can't accomplish all the things he needs to do each year without a lot of assistance from some very special people. We would like to extend our gratitude and thanks to all of our helpers who made this book possible.

First, a huge thank you to our families and friends for their tireless support and encouragement. Special thanks to Jim's wife, Kelly, who in the midst of doubt and rejection reminded him of the book's inherent worth and its ability to brighten even the darkest spirit. And thanks to Jim's parents and grandparents for providing him the gift of believing in the essence of Santa Claus.

A special thank you from Carl to the management and staff of NorthPark Center in Dallas. These tireless elves have offered "Santa" continuous support and have worked diligently to create a warm and wonderful, magical home-away-from-home for him to personally receive the heartfelt wishes, letters and lists of some 100,000 children in the past decade.

Carl would also like to thank his parents and family for their ongoing encouragement, support and understanding.

Without the conviction, encouragement and guidance of the good people at our publisher, Health Communications, Inc., this collection of children's letters would not have found its way into your hands. Special thanks to Peter Vesgo, Allison Janse, Christine Belleris, Matthew Diener, Lisa Drucker, Kim Weiss, Kelly Maragni, Randee Goldsmith, Larissa Hise and all of the wonderful employees at HCI for seeing the "magic" in the book's concept and making it a reality.

Our hearts go out in thanks to the following special friends, collaborators and supporters—"Santa's Helpers" in the best sense of the words: Nancy, David and Sarah, Billy, Cody and Lori, Linda and Jordan, Ann and crew, Meg (from the beginning), John, Charles, Sharon, Stan, Sandra and Bob, Gloria and Mike, Sheryl and Dave, Jewel, Saundra, Connie and Bill, Cheryl and Dal, Lisa and Dean, Lisa and Andy, Jody and Bob, Jo and Sully (and Miss Jenny), Allison, Jenny H. and Rudolph (of course).

Grateful thanks and special recognition go to Willie Russell with the Department of Education Program at the main U.S. Post Office in Dallas, and to Andy Sozzi with the Corporate Relations Department at the U.S. Post Office in New York City for their generosity.

A final thanks goes to all the children (and their parents, grandparents, and custodians) who take pen, pencil, crayon, and keyboard in hand each year, open their hearts, and share with us their most secret wishes and dreams. We love and appreciate you all.

Introduction

The first child who sat on my lap was a curly headed five-year-old boy. He made himself comfortable, looked me right in the eye and said, "My Daddy left us and moved to Waco. I guess he doesn't love us anymore." I realized then that, as Santa, I was going to hear about a lot more than which G.I. Joe or Barbie doll children wanted for Christmas.

Since 1983, I have had the unique opportunity to personify Santa Claus in a variety of settings. I quickly learned to keep a journal with me, as the children's visits were filled with moments of warmth, humor and poignancy. Of course, as I wrote in the journals, the children thought I was dutifully noting every detail of the fire truck or video games they were requesting. In fact, I might have been writing that they asked, "What do you and Mrs. Claus fight about?" or, that in regards to being good, they said, "I don't bite, kick or plug things in," or "Sometimes I was bad, but those times were just a joke. Do you have to tell the elves?"

What happens when a child visits or communicates with Santa can sometimes be like a snapshot—a brief glimpse of his or her life. Santa has heard a young boy ask for a toy microphone so that his parents can hear him when they are fighting. A little girl hoped to see her grandmother for Christmas—Santa learned that grandma passed away that year and was greatly missed.

The intensity and genuineness of emotion associated with many children's belief in Santa have been impressive and surprising. These feelings are also revealed in their lists and letters, such as those in this collection. The letters come in all sizes, shapes, styles, colors and formats. They might be as brief as a few wanted toys scribbled on a napkin or the back of a parent's business card while waiting in line, or quite lengthy and formal. I've received more than one elaborately constructed "book" containing the child's wishes, adorned with drawings and pictures. The record stands at an eighty-four page tome filled with carefully cut-out pictures (from various advertisements and store catalogs) of everything one seven-year-old thought he deserved.

The letters may be written in a barely decipherable scrawl (sometimes accompanied by a parent's translation) or, alas, increasingly they may be projected in the latest high-tech computer-aided format. Fortunately, no child has yet simply handed over or mailed in a disk, floppy or otherwise. Some letters are little more than a simple listing of hoped-for toys. Others can be quite chatty and comprehensive. They might give helpful advice or let Santa know that this year instead of milk and cookies, he can expect "Cheetos and a beer." (A father's helpful influence is detected here.)

Many letters contain declarations of affection and appreciation. It is clear that children feel loved by Santa and they return that sentiment. As one young man put it, "It's good for kids to know that there's someone like Santa who cares for them and wants them to be happy." Children can express themselves through a simple "I love you Santa" or through very detailed pictures. Of course, all such artwork is displayed in the special children's gallery at the North Pole.

A difficult aspect of representing Santa is that because he has special powers, he is sometimes asked to accomplish the impossible. These requests most often take the form of helping a relative or friend who is sick or suffering in some way to get better, or even pleas to find a lost pet. In person, I can respond to these situations by acknowledging the child's feelings and being clear about the limits of Santa's abilities. Such letters when received, unfortunately, often fail to contain an address or other way to reach the child.

Children are also very curious and awed by every aspect of Santa's life, and their letters and visits contain unique questions. A big source of concern for the children is how Santa manages to do all he does, especially at the child's house, "We don't have a chimney. How will you get in?", "How do you bring puppies on the sleigh?" and, "How do you get all around the world in one night?".

Some of the letters and lists included in this compilation were collected over my sixteen-year career as Santa, during which time I have seen approximately 140,000 children. Other letters were gathered directly from the United States Post Offices in New York and Dallas by my collaborator Jim Walker Jr.

A Scandinavian heritage has blessed me with bushy blond-white hair and beard, a stocky physique, reddish cheeks and blue eyes that have been said to twinkle. Thus my portrayal of the jolly St. Nick has been "natural" (i.e., unaided by make-up or padding). In addition to my informal study of Santa through personal experience, he was also the subject of my doctoral dissertation at the University of Texas at Austin. Currently I am a licensed psychologist, an adjunct faculty member of UT, and a professional storyteller, children's entertainer and speaker.

My portrayals of Santa Claus began in 1983 at NorthCross and Highland Malls in Austin, Texas. From there I moved to Santa Monica Place in Santa Monica, California. From 1989 to the present I have been at NorthPark Center in Dallas, Texas.

The extended stay in Dallas has been particularly beneficial and rewarding. The management and staff of NorthPark Center have done everything possible to create an elaborate, distinctively beautiful and magical setting for children and their families to visit Santa. Mothers and teachers have shared with me that according to playground and preschool lore in Dallas, the "real" Santa is at NorthPark. As a result, Santa has developed a loyal following of children who come each year, resulting in a unique opportunity to maintain and renew connections with the children. Each year as the season progresses the walls of my dressing room become covered with selected letters. These letters and lists, and adult reactions to them became the original inspiration for this book.

In reviewing the letters, they seemed to fall naturally into categories and are arranged accordingly into five sections, each with a very brief introduction. Some of the original letters are reproduced in their entirety in the children's own handwriting with their creative wording, spelling and limitations, the most intriguing aspects have been excerpted.

Santa is perceived and experienced by children in a manner reflective of who they are. For some he is a consistently loving father figure; others are awed and amazed by his magic. Older children may relate to him as a playful companion and old friend. He is a keeper of secrets and a living representation of hope and the belief that dreams do come true. For all of these reasons and more, children openly express themselves to Santa and touch his heart. Enjoy your peek into the special connection between children and the jolliest of the midwinter gift-givers as revealed in this initial collection of *All I Want for Christmas Is . . . Letters from Santa's Mailbag.*

Carl Anderson, Ph.D.

1

What I Want for Christmas and Some Special Instructions

Getting a clear picture of what a child wants for Christmas is not always easy. It can be unclear if there really is a "yellow teddy bear that talks when you brush your teeth." There are also surprises such as the two-year-old who wanted only "candy and diamonds," or the ninety-years-young great-grandmother who wanted "a new boyfriend, 'cause mine's too old; and I'm too old to worry about being good anymore!"

While some lists are long, most children know to expect only one or two special treats from Santa and the most important items are often indicated by stars, underlining or other creative means of emphasis.

There are also special instructions such as: notification that the family will be visiting out-of-town relatives on Christmas and where they can be found; what kind of snack Santa might expect to receive; and even a request for Santa to be a little neater this year by not tracking as much soot from the chimney through the house, or to "pick up after the reindeer. Last year they pooped on the driveway." It is a good thing Santa makes lists, he has so much to keep up with.

"I want a pair of real crutches and a real cast."

"Twelve books that I will always want to read."

"I want at least 1,000 baseball cards. I quote 'baseball cards'."

"I would like a tell-a-scoop. If it takes all year to make it just buy it."

"I want a Ken doll with a head on it."

"No thank you for the fruit."

"Please bring me a pig, a Christmas angel and a trip to the North Pole."

"If you don't now what some of these things are you can see what it is in Learn and play Magazien."

Dear Santa,

Don't forget to bring your tools so you can take the top off of our chimney.

From Mark

Dear Santa,

Please watch out for my cat,

he sleeps under the tree.

Love,

Angela

Dear Santa Claus,

  You know thet song "All I want for Christmas are Two Front Teeth." Well that's not what I want. All I want is *my* Family and Friends. But there is one thing I want to know are you real?

Sincerely,

Aida

Dear Santa,

I would like to have anything you can give me.

Love,
Ally

Dear Santa,

I know your kind of busy right now getting every theng ready for Christmas but do you thenk you could bring my momy home for Christmas. I'm realy sorry for saying that I don't believe in you, but I do. I'm not ask for me. I'm asking because It won't be the same without her, and my dady is very lonley.

Love Your Believer

Billy

P.S. I'm not going to set a trap.

Dear: Santa Claus,

I'm 9 years old. I'm Sorry To Desturb You With This Letter, But If Your Not to Busy, I Would Like to Ask You For A Kitten For Christmas. My Mom Might Not Let Me Keep It In The House, So I'll Beg Her And Try The Sad Puppy Face, So I Can Keep It In My room At All Times. I Just wanted To Ask For A Kitten. If I Can't have A Kitten, I Don't Want ANYTHING!, For Christmas

P.S. I Know I'v Done A Lot Of Bad Things, But I'll try to be Better and I Hope You Don't Die, "EVER!"

Dear Santa Claus,

Here is my Christmas List. I hope you get it. I'm not giving a command but the things on my list I want what ever you could give me on the list if not I will take something different. Exept a spiting and peeing, talking doll.

Thank You

Love You

Merry Christmas.

Love

Sara

Name: Karen

Thing I what from Santa for

Christmas

1. May I have a bike just like I have

now but a 20 inch bike please.

2. I wish that one day mommy and

daddy will get married please.

3. I wish to live in a house with

mommy and daddy please.

4. I wish mommy and daddy quit fight.

I want
a world
that
is happy
And a
teddy bear.
Love Alyssa

Dear Santa,

I know your really busy but please read this ok. What I really want for Christmas is nothing at all. You may ask why. The reason is I have not been good at all the hole year. So anything you got for me take it back or give it to a kid that needs it. So please don't get me anything for Christmas well give me some cole and swiches,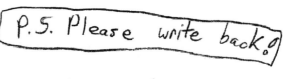

P.S. Please write back?

yours Turely
Emily

Dear Santa,

I know my parents don't realy want this, but the only thing I want this Christmass is for my cat (Millie) to have kittens. If it's asking too much, I would like the father to be a white persion.

Your very good friend,

David

p.s. These kittens are very special to me.

Dear Santa Claus,

I was wondering if you could get me a puppy for Christmas this year. I'll take care of it. I Promise. You should know I already had one before. My father mainly took care of it. That was one big dog. Oh all I want is a puppy. That is all I want.

P.S. Some say your not real, But if this happens I believe that you are real.

Jasmin

Merry Christmas!

Dear Santa,

Can I please be one of

your elves.

DeAr   SANtA,
I hAve Been
pretty goOD
this   yeAr
I woulD like
A Big shiny
red new bike
that hAs DOts
like uncle Hectors
CAr please

love MychAel

Dear Santa,

I want some poker chips but I won't gambell I swear to God and Jeus. I also want a remot control car but you can bring anything but if you have enough room in your sliegh you may bring them. With some Batman figures please. How are you and Mrs. Claus have a Merry X-Mas.

Love,
Dustin

P.S. Will you give the poor a home.
P.P.S. Bring $80.00 please.

Dear Santa Claus

I have been a very good girl this year. Tommorrow Christmas Eve is my Birth day and I will get no presents this year because my mother lost her job and my father just left us and my mother cries a lot and I fell so bad Would you please send me and my sister a pressent a doodle Bear and a cadage Patch doll).

I love you santa

Arielle

Dear Santa,

I want Jake the brown monkey (he is at the Hallmark store) I hid him in the back where the stuffed animals are in a pile under the shelves with stuffed animals on him.

Thank you,

Corey

Dear Santa I like your songs and all the

presents you give to the childrn.
but all I want is a dog
like Albert for Christmas
because I loved him so much
I thought that I was the
luckiest girl on Earth because
I had Albert

from Nicollette.

Dear Santa,

I would like a Red Dragon, and if possible some Power Ranger figurines. Please deliver to Illinois, I will be at Gramma's house.

Love, Jordan

PS. Bring my new sister some presents, too.

Dear Santa Clas What I want far Chrismas is All My famely together On Chrismas day and Ohpin presins together to On Chrismas Morning. p.s. I'll leve Some CholitChip Chokse On the tabe by the Chibrey.

from. ehlee

Mary Chirsmas to all and good night Ho! Ho! Ho!

Dear Santa I want a barbie gEEp anp a a new Baby brother anp a ringset anp a baThrob so I wont get cold win I get out of The BaThtub I am so sorry That i have Ben men to my parinst

Love kaxia

Dear Santa Claus,

My name is Haley I can't afford

money to buy a coat for winter. Winter

is almost coming, and I don't have a

coat at all please I love you very much I

know people don't believe I you but I do,

my size is 12 for my cost please I do

believe in you, love you.

Love Haley

Dear Santa Claus, Do you really come down the chimmery Santa? Well I guess I better tell you that I want Computer games here are their manes and rating on a scale 1-10 tie Freighter 9. War Craft 9, Mist 9, NHL Hockey 4, and the one where you destroy robots. I want a Mountain Bike with 10 gears and that looks coll. The things I want most are all the computer games that I tried at Laser-X yes even the golf game.

Now, can you tell me a few answers to these questions? Please put the answers in my stocking. What are the other reindeers names? Who are your favorite elves? What time do you do you start out? Who do you think has been better just for the record me or Cortney? These are all the questions I have. The thing I would like to know the most is what will you put in my stocking? Will it be a race car but nothing to big because I am going on a cruise. It will be great because it is recommended by a big association. There will be Looney Tunes on board. These are all the things I want for Christmas. This also what I am doing for Christmas. By the way go down the living room chimney. It is gas fireplace and it will be off.

Your Friend, Scott

P.S. I hope you like my list because it is 251 words.

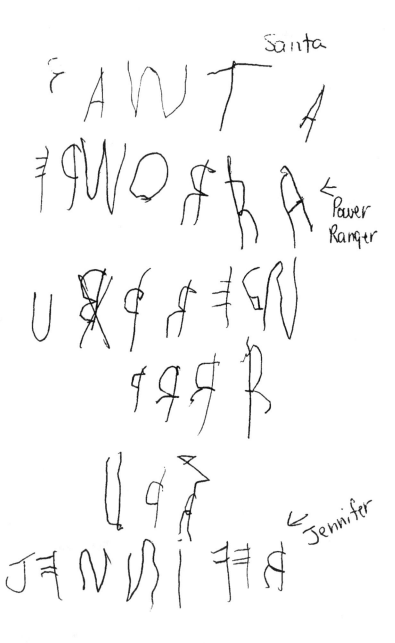

Dear Santa,

What I really want for
Christmas is my dad permission
that all four of my sisters could
paint are nails.

Your Friend,

Laura

Dear Santa,

Hi Santa! You need to get a fax machine so I can fax my letter to you each year. That way, if I send it really late, it will get there real soon. Also, when you get the fax, mail me you phone number. That would be real nice of you. It would also be great if you got a secret website, and make a special password for me. You can mail it with the fax and phone number. Please tell all the reindeer I love them.

Love Tabitha

P.S. Ask Mrs. Clause to send some of her yummy cookies.

Dear Santa Claus,

My name is Shaundra and I'm 12 year old. I have a sister and she is 7 years old. I live in the poorest boro in New York, The Bronx. I just want to say if you could give me a big smile this Christmas,

Merry Christmas,

Thank You,

Yours truly. Shaundra

Dear Santa
Nick wants a truck
and a farm and a Big
Car Carrier and a Drum
and a Grocery Basket Set
and Mortal KomBat
I'am wrtieing this note
for my little bother
becuse hie does not Know how
to wrtie

your friend,
Nevana

Dear Santa Clause,

How are you doing? I am fine. On Christmas Eve can you please give us presents? Because we are going to New York Very early in the morning and no one wants to wake up even earlier on Christmas.

Thank You

Mary

P.S. To tell you the truth I was not a very good girl this year I'm sorry.

P.S.S. I'll understand If I wont get presents on Christmas Eve.

Dear Santa,

I know you are true because I wrote a Note to you last year and you wrote Back. I am in 3rd grade right now. We have a Parrot and a dog. My dogs' name is Chico. I think my dog is going to be inside. So please watch out because my dog doesn't like Stranger. I belive that you got magic My mom said, "Thata Santa has Magic." So use your magic. I might Leave you some cookies and milk. And please write Back.

Love
Olivia

Dear Santa, I wos a good bowey thes yer. I wont a pocet nife and a crepeye crolrs set weth evreytheg that came weth it. Wey wel leve sum coceys and milk. For you From, Robert

Dear Santa,

What I want for Christmas is a girl

Chawawa to have puppys it's okay

with my mom, The barbie McDana

Rastarunt, the baby alive that really

cries and lots of candy canes, and my

size barbie.

Love,

Kelly

p.s. Everythings okay with my mom.

Dear Santa I

~~Cha~~ Changed

~~My~~ ~~My~~n~~d~~

Minde I Whants

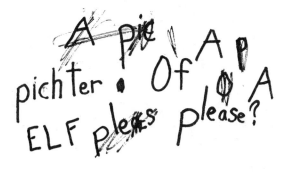

~~A pie~~ A

pichter · Of A

ELF ~~pless~~ please?

Dear Santa,

For Christmas I would like a shetland sheepdog. Could it be a male? And could it be grown up?

Love,

Allie

P.S. We love you.

Dear Santa Claus,

I want for Christmas a Nano Baby, Gigapet, Keyboard, Computer, Bike, Turtle doves, Athletic stuff, grandpa to stop yelling, and craft stuff.

Love,

Julie

P.S. I've been good, Haven't I?

Dear Santa Claus,

I want a white teddy bear
with black nose and eyes.
Please put a big red bow
around his neck. Also, I would
like a bunny with a railroad
drivers suit and cap.

Thank you Love,

Megan

Merry Christmas

Dear Santa,

I want a little people dollhouse with a gym and a grandma's house. That's all I want.

Love, Alissa

Santa,
Alissa's parents thought she wanted a Playskool Dollhouse can your elves help?

Dear Santa,

I want a camera, a remote control car, a BB gun, some firecrackers, and most of all I want a Nintendo 64. If you don't get it you'll be sorry. I know where the North Pole is. We looked it up at school. Its above Canada. <u>Bring it to me or we'll have Prancer burgers tonight!</u> I'm not kidding. The grill is cook'n!

Jeremy

P.S. Mom says we might be in Denver.

DEAR SANTA,

AM I ON THE GOOD LIST OR THE BAD LIST? IF I AM ON THE GOOD LIST, I WANT SOME BLUE SLIPPERS AND A BLUE ROBE AND A FEW SURPRISES. I WOULD ALSO LIKE A COWBOY ROBE FOR MY BROTHER SO THAT I CAN GIVE IT TO HIM. I HATE IT WHEN HE COMES OUT OF THE BATHROOM NAKED. THE REASON WHY I AM ASKING YOU IS BECAUSE I DON'T HAVE ANY MONEY. IF I AM ON THE BAD LIST, PLEASE DON'T GIVE ME TOO MUCH COAL.

THANK YOU,

REBECCA

Wishes and
Requests from
the Heart

The rituals relating to Santa Claus have been criticized for contributing to a sense of greed and materialism surrounding the Christmas holiday. Many children grasp, however, the symbolic lessons regarding charitable giving and thinking of others that Santa and the season teach. This comprehension is reflected in their wishes for gifts or better situations or health for family and friends, and also for the world in general. Many letters include and some contain only a wish for someone else, or for the poor, the sick, or the needy to be remembered or helped in some fashion. Even the youngest children seem to know that it is okay to wish for a new bike and world peace at the same time.

Children also ask sometimes for the relief of painful personal feelings they may be having such as grief, loneliness or feeling mistreated and powerless. A sense of hope may be the most important gift Santa brings to children.

 "I only want one thing this year—a sister!"

 "I want peace to the world, and no fighting and maybe, if you can, a bike."

"Please everybody have a good Christmas. Everybody that doesn't have anything gets something."

" . . . the most speclies thaing of all to get my grandmother to get well. Please! Please! Please!"

"I don't care if you ferget some things that I want. Just get some things for my perrents."

"Most of all I want a tiny puppy because my dog ran away and never came back! I just want someone to cuddle and play with."

"Please give my family and I happiness and joy through the year and let them be happy on Christmas day. I bet they'l be very thoughtful and kind to give me presents so you don't have to worry."

"All I want for Christmas is for my mom to be happy. NO PRESENTS!!!! I am 9 years old."

 "You can forget all the toys this year. What I would like most of all is for my brother to get better, recover from his stroke and speak and act like he used to and not have to take pills all the time."

Dear Santa,

Help find our kitty if you can.

Help him get home in time for

Christmas, and you can rap him

in a box if you want.

Love,

Kristin

Dear beloving Santa,
I have some wishes
that had never comed
true and you are my last
hope. Here are my wishes:
I wish that my mom
wont have seasers and
have to go to the
hospital again.
    I wish that my
tored vane would stop
bleeding. I don't want
toys I just want that
for christmas.
                Sincerely,
                Mary

Dear Santa,

   I Love you Santa I now there

are lots of kids out there that

Do not have iney toy's so if

you Do not hav unaf of toy's

pleys giv those ones that Do

not hav toy's

                    Love Breanne

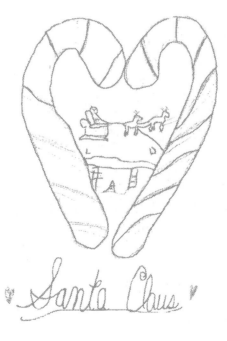

Dear Santa Claus,

I am writing this letter for my little cousin. She and her mother are very poor. They didn't have a Christmas dinner, or no presents at all my cousin wants is a new winter coat and a nice dinner with cake. She is 10 yrs old and handicapped so she goes to a special school But this year She and her mother just moved out here in October and she didn't get to go to the Christmas or see Santa Claus. A teacher comes to her house and teaches her. Can you please help Christmas came and Left no gifts for her. I love her very much

David

Dear Santa Claus,
I hope you
Can deliver
all your

toys in one
Night. If

you need any
help, call me

Love, Brooks

Dear Santa,

   This is what I want for Christmas. I would like a boom box and a bike and that me and my friends never get in a fight. I've tryed to be really good this year. The reason I did'n ask for a lot is because I think friendship is better than presants.

Signed,

Sharley

Dear Santa Clause,

I know this might sound kind of weird, but I wanted to ask you if you would come to my house and pick me up on Mondays, Tuesdays, and Wednesdays after school.

I don't want us to go to my baby sisters house so I thought you might take me to your house. There is one more question that I wanted to ask you. Will you send me anything that will teach me to fly.

Your friend,
Drew

Dear Santa:

I'm 17 year's old and a senior in high school. Well, this Christmas isn't going to be so good! But I was kind of hoping that I could ask for a "watch" for Christmas. Before my father died he bought me a Mickey Mouse watch, but in Ceramics class, someone stole it!

I believe, who ever stole it, had no clue, that my father bought it for me! But as soon as I wore it, everyday, every hour, and every minute! I felt as if, he (my dad) was with me, every second, of my day! Well Santa, I hope my wish can come true! Thank You so much for making my every wish from the past, come true!

Love always.
Helen

Dear Santa

I WANT
my DAD<u>Dy</u>.

Dear Saint Nick,

Thank you ever so much for the keyboard I play it every time I go to my dad's. I especially like the "waw voice." It's sort of like a music tone. Well, I hope Mrs. Claus and all the elves are fine. They probably don't get much attention around Christmas. Well, at least not Mrs. Claus. (That was not meant in a mean way but serious way.)

Savannah

Dear Santa,

I want Peace on Earth and my

little sister from bothering me.

From

Ryan

Dear Santa,

How are you and Mrs. Clause? I am Fine! I am also doing good in school this year! I made a 95% in my overall score For the First nine weeks. I've got into a little bit of trouble at school, but other than that I've been pretty good. How are your raindeer? Are they all right? I hope so. I know I'm 11 years old now but please don't stop comeing to my house. I know Christmas is not just that Santa Clause comes and you get presents it is to celebrate Christ's birth. I really like what you brought me last year. Here are a few things that I'd like for Christmas this year First I'd like it if you could send the nicest clothes and shoes to the kids in Korea, China, Africa, and Mexico. I'd like some Roller blades and the pads and stuff. This year instead of Barbie clothes and gum, could you give me a pair of new Nikes with extra glue on the soles. Santa I am going to try to leave hay out for your raindeer. We have an alarm sestem so be careful O.K.. Here is Cheryl's list she can't spell yet so I need to write for her next year you may get a letter From me and Cheryl. Cheryl wants a new barbie, and a trampalen, Walkietalkies.

                    Love Lindsay and Cheryl

P.S. Please write back!

Dear Santa,

Can you get Mommy and

Daddy back together again?

Thank you,

Elisabeth

Dear Santa,

   I would like an automatic paintball gun for Christmas. I know I haven't written you in a while and I'm very sorry, but I hope you'll understand that I find it very hard to get time to write you.

                  Sincerely

                  Travis

P.S. I'll be careful when I'm playing Paintball.

Dear Santa,

For Christmas I would like a ninteno 64 and a toy cherry red viper and also I want you to give my mom and Dad some money we do not have (money) I want my dad to be happy and bring my mom a GMC SAFFri and help my sister to get well from Atism.

Thank you
Carlos

Dear Santa Claus,

I have been good almost half of the year. I have a wish but it never came true. Can you make me wish came true. My wish is that my dad can dot get sick no more.

Your friend.

Melissa

Dear Santa,
I have written this note to tell you something. My mom needs a bike to ride on. I saw one and thought I'd tell you about it. It is a red huffy.
It has big, balloon tires, bent handlebars, one speed gear, old-looking frame, coiled spring seats, and a leather seat.
I saw it at Tom Thumb. It cost $119.00*tax

Please?

Dear Santa,

My name is Alex. I am 10 years old. We are very poor. We don't live with my Father because he is divorced of my mother. I live with my mother and my two brothers Jose (4 years) and Manny. (5 years) Our dream is to have a Nintendo. My mother is too Poor. That she can't buy us things we need like food or closes. Sometime we are starving, without food to eat. You know that I miss my father and you too. Sometime we cry because we miss my father and you. I want what you think is good for us.

Jose	Manny	Me
Pants 7	7	5/6
Shoes $12^1/_2$	$13^1/_2$	7

Dear Santa,

Will you let dad spean time with us I need your help. You're the only one.

Love,

Beth

P.S. your the greatest

Dear Santa,
Can you please
get my mom
something
she wants
to make her
feel better.
Thank you.
Love,
Ashley

Dear Santa,

For Christmas I want some new shoes. And I want our truth to come back to us. And a little chick. And we want us to be healthy for the rest of our life. And how are you doing? I'm doing fine. I hope you don't get to tired. I'm going to leave milk and cookies if I have any. "Okay!" And you can grant me this last wish? Would you give the power to my big sister to make her talk?

Pleeeaaassseee!

Sincerely,

Erica

P.S. Merry Christmas Santa.

Dear Santa
all I want for
chrsmas is for
my baby coisen,
Brandn, to get
better.

Tiffany

Dear Santa,

    I Love you Santa

    Merry Christmas

    All I wish is to see

    my Grandpa for

    Christmas

    Please for me.

                Mallory

Dear Santa,

This is my full list of things I want for Christmas. My own ice skates, a foot print of all your reindeer, rudolph's can be in red. An artificial Christmas tree, my dad to be happy, a puppy.

Love, Charlotte

Dear Santa

Will you please give each dog and cat

neckstor a good home or try to. I relly

want a pony, or Horse. How are you?

Dose enyone (or enythig) hav the flu?

Melissa

P.S. Merry Chismus

Dear Santa Claus

My dad is in gail and I am so sad because his not going to be with us this Christmas and we are not going to have presents like last year I live with my ant in her house and my two uncels and my mom and all I am asking is for some presents, a mountain bike and the other things are in the envelope thank you Santa I hope my dad was with us I am sad

Size of pants 12-14

Size of shirt L

Size of shoes $6^{1}/2$

Jacket M

Dear Santa,

Please bring all the sick kids a toy or a book and something to eat.

Love,
Morgan Elizabeth

Dear Santa Claus,
my Friends don't believe
in You So I Want You
to give me a picture of
Rudolph

Dear Santa

I want a SkateBoard

I want a rollerBlades

I want a voiceactivater remote

control

I want a footBall

I want my family to have Healthy

Bodies.

Name Lawrence.

Dear Santa North

I live in a apartment I don't have a chimney but if you can't get the presents in my house send me back a letter. Now for the list all tell you wat I want for Furtere threespawn toys ten spitermantoys three games For PlayStotronteKen2and2andSyleEgeIalways wanted to the WWW. Thing on the computer but I dont now how so I want I conputer that when it starts ill say Adress then I can do the WWW. Thing. I want my brothers to act good intede bad I want two Frieds living in my hose forever. My mom and dad smoke a drik to much so please stop them From smokin were poor and don't have that much food or money so we coud need that I have a front about something so you can stop that help my hole Family have a batter life anf hafe a mery mery Chistmas

Love

Robby

Dear Santa,

My name is Lucas and I am 10 yrs. Old. My brother 9 years can you please send us some clothes for Christmas. My mother is a widow and she does not have enough money to boy us clothes. My size in pants is 36 and shirts large. My brother sizes in pants is 32 and medium in shirts.

Thank you for you time and Corporation

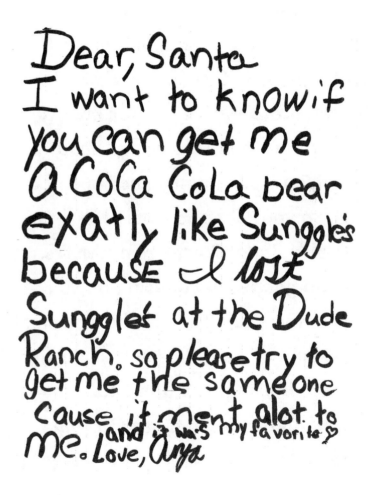

Dear, Santa
I want to knowif
you can get me
a CoCa CoLa bear
exatly like Sunggles
because I lost
Sunggles at the Dude
Ranch. so pleasetry to
get me the same one
Cause it ment alot to
me. and it was my favorite ♥
Love, Anya

Dear Santa,

I wish you could come to visit me. This is what I want for Christmas: A computer, a new bike, a barbie, and four extra presents. One for my Dad, Mother, brother, and one for my big brother. Santa please bring these presents to me. I really need them! Say Hello, to your elves for me! I like Rudolph's song. Do the reindeer treat Rudolph good? I'm counting on you Santa. If you don't make this for me, I will be kind of sad! Please make my dad to stop drinking, but don't talk to him. Since I guana died I've been acting crazy. Well, Santa MERRY CHRISTMAS!!

Sincerely,

Lauren

Dear Santa,

Last year Andrew asked for a Koala back pack from you but not mom and dad. He now kind of doubts you're the real McCoy. Could you let him know you just ran out of those last year?

Thanks

DAD

Dear Santa,

These buttons came off my

Buzz Lightyear I thought you

could use them to make

another boy a new Buzz

                           Alexander

Dear Santa Clause,

My name is Brian. I am 10 years old. I live with my mother, father, and my other Brother Richie. He is 13 years old.

This year has been very sad. My father is not making money; my Mother takes care of us. She cannot work because my brother needs to be cared for.

Please Santa can you do me favor and please bring my brother Richie some soft toys. He is mentaly Retarded and he doesn't talk so I can't ask him what he wants, but he throws things and my mother is always scared he'll hurt someone. He likes stuff animals and he likes toys that talk.

Thank you very much.
Richie and Brian

Dear Santa Claus,

I want a picture of my Grandpa. He died before I was born. He is my mom's dad but he died. I wish I could see him in a picture. Every thing else you can surprise. Please no strange things O.K.

P.S. If you can't get a picture of him now you can you try to leave a picture from long ago. Please.

A Note For Santa

November 28

Dear, Santa

There is just 2 gifes I won't for
Christmas ths year. The 2 gifes I
won't are: a computer, and a pair of
glasses. The computer is for my
flamily, but it's mosty for my mom. It's
mosty for my mom because she has to
grade 3 classes work. The glasses
are for me to see better because I
have a hard time seeing the board
where I set. In my homeroom and I
set in the very back. In math class I
set in the frount and I still can't see.

P.S. Please get me both things Santa.

On Being Good, Appreciation and Affection

Most children know not to worry too much about being good for Santa. He assures them that he knows they are good by nature, and that they will get tired or grumpy or uncooperative from time-to-time, but so do grown-ups and even elves. It's tradition, however, to let Santa know that one has been good and in what way, and if not, why not. Comments and excuses are often hilarious, and reveal future politicians in the making: "Was I good? Do you mean today or, like, all year?"

Children can also be the most spontaneously appreciative and affectionate of us all, and anyone who has had the special opportunity to experience this outpouring of love by portraying Santa will attest to how rewarding it can be. With children, there is no doubt that their feelings come straight from the heart.

 "Santa, you know how I was being polite. I was not just doing that cause I was coming to see you."

 "Thank you Santa for all you do for me. I love my penguin. His name is Butch."

 "I realy luv you wil you bee my friend?"

 "Some people say you arernt the real Santa and some people say theres no such thing as Santa. Evein if you arent the real Santa I think you are making a lot of kids happy."

🍬 "Come visit us someday after Christmas if you want to !!!"

🍬 "My dad says thanks for the football that you gave him in 1964."

🍬 "I try not to pick on my brother, but its hard."

🍬 "Im sending you gift because of all the hard work of sending every kid and every animal a gift so I love you Santa Clause and keep watching me!"

🍬 "Roses ar red, Vilits are blue, snow is cold, but we like you."

🍬 "This is from girl with lipstick stuck in her hair. I love you Santa."

🍬 "I wish I could see you but I know I'm not supposed to. The one I go to looks just like you. I love you."

🍬 "I am glad elves can make presents."

Dear Santa,

I should't get as many gifts as I usaully do, I've been too much of a smart allec. (If it's okay with you.) Please say hi to Mrs. Claus for me.

Merry Christmas!

From, Katie

Dear Santa
My sitter Elzzabeth
has been bad this
year,

Dear Santa,

Mommy and daddy say I haven't been too good this year. Sometines they aren't too good either. I would like a new Barbie and some new clothes. Really anything will be fine. Stay warm. I love you.

Love,

Jessica

Dear Santa I belive
in elves becouse they
make toys for chlidren
and I belive in you to.
    BY Santa
    AND A HAPPY
    NEW YEAR
      LOVE
    KRISTIN
    AND CAN I POEL
    ON YOUR BUERD

Dear Santa,

I think I know how you fill of everuyody giving you letters. Will today you are going to see a different letter now lets git on with it. My mom has been good.

My dad has been good.

Win I be bad enough to git coal can you please poot letter on it and poot wat I shofdon. My mom sed you sometimes you come down to earth to be santa. A person did't baleeve in you. I saw the same grl she dost git presents. The reason I did it through the mail is because I whonid to be you. Now I will tell you what I want for christmas. A big magic stroller baby.

Love
Jennifer

Dear Santa,

I've been bad. Please bring me coal. I thank you.

Your friend,

Chris

Dear Santa,

For Christmas, I would like a Diary, Roller Blades and Staci Barbies nifty little sisters. Please will you hold all the practical stuff.

Love,

Stefanie

P.S. I have not been a perfect little girl but I have been very good. (I am not lying).

Dear Santa,

My name is Amber, I am 11 years old. I'll turn 12 in August. This year I've tried to be really good, but I have two smaller brothers one younger sister and you know how tough that is. I have a lot of thing, But I really want is 1 or 2 gingy pigs. I love animals. I only have 2, one dog and a cat. My dog's name is black eyed bumper. We call him Bumpr for short. My cats name is oliver. That's really all I want.

P.S. I still belive in you!!!!

Dear Santa Claus,

This year I want a......

What do I want? Something special...can you think of something? Oh yeah stuffed animal and a surprise. (I like suprises!) I have been a little bad, altough I'd rather not admit it (1) I looked inside a present (2) I left cookies, carrots,turnovers

TO: Santa
Cluase

Chris
Crinckle

Dear Santa,
   I have been a bad girl this year.
I have lied, stole money, and I fight, and I
have been notty. I wish I couldgoto
church and I wish you will forgive me.
I hope all children are safe. Will
you forgive me please!!!!

                    love,
                    Michalle

Dar Santa,

I have been good but my brother has been beter then me. But still could you give me some presints for X-Mas. I want China tea set, ragedeann, a rell Elf of yors, A red X-Mas dress, A rell pupy.

THE END

Dear Santa,

I have been very good this year. I've said some bad words this year, but none today. I've minded my Mom and Dad. I have not kicked the dog. For Christmas this year I would like:

- Electronic guitar like I saw at the party store
- Orange football
- Pug mug and pencils
- Tools: monkey wrench, screwdriver, hammer
- Legos: Skeleton Surprise and Blizzard baron
- Remote control fire chief car
- Curious George books
- A real live Pug puppy
- Mighty Maz: Vamp Biter, Lava Best, Wolfship 7, Palace of Poison

Love,
Dietrich

Dear santol,

We will be at
Granama A
house for christm
as My name is
marc
I've been
good to day

Dear Santa,

I would like to have a grown-up sleeping bag a tamagotia, and maybe an outfit.

I have tried to be good all year but I haven't succeeded real well. Sorry if I mispelled.

Love, Morgan

I know santa that you may not git a prisent from any boty but I want you to know that even thow you dount fit a prisent but you are actually receiving one from me because I want you to undersdand that I love you and I thing you are a wonderful man santa so this message I want you to rummber and keep it in your hart.

So dount fergit me!

I ♥ you

Dear st. Nicholas

I am sorry for the times I been

Bad this year. From now on I'll

be good and never do it again.

I hope you don't pass my

heuse.

From Jozef

Merry Christmas
Santa I Hope You
Like Chocolate Chip
Cookies and
Egg nog.
Some of the kids
in my class don't
belive in you and say
mean things about
you but not me I love you and I belive in
you! Ho Ho Ho and thanks for my
trapolein it's great!

Dear Santa I know I have not ben the best I can be I think my attitude has not ben god these past three weeks. I don't know what happened I done things like telling stories being bad in school not doing my work hitting my brothers. And will try to improve in all the things mostly being bad to my family. But I need help so could you help me in some way. Even tho I haven't ben the best I can be would please give the flowing!!!!!!

1. A PLAYSTATION WITH GAMES!!!!!
2. TOMMY HILFIGER SHIRTS AND SHOES MY FAVORITE COLOR IS RED!!!!
3. NEW ROLLER BLADES!
4. NEW BIKE!!!
5. JEWELRY!!!!
6. THE NEW PENNY HARDYWAY SHOES!!!!!
7. A VERY VERY BIG SONY RADIO!!
8. Close like tommy, natica and polo
9. WORLD PEACE!!!!!!!!!!!!!!!!!!!!!!

Sincerely Paula

Dear Santa,

How are you? I am Evan and I want a Batman Shooter for Christmas. I be good tomarrow and until Christmas.

Love you,

Evan

Dec. 12

Dear santa clause,

I've been doing stuff I really shouldn't be like stealing and othere stuff like lying. I hope if you have in your heart to for give me and these are the stuff I would like well it not that much.

I would like probbly stuff like a

football

racecare

basketball

super man toys

roller blades

clothes

Hand Held game

Love,
Gustavo

Dear Santa and mrs. Claus,

I have tried to be nice to my brother but I don't have much patients with him that's why we get in fights a lot. I hope you can forgive me. I have been kindy bad but not really I don't think. If you think I have been bad I will try to be nicer. Is it cold up there? How is the reindeer? Have a great christmas.

Love,

Lexi

P.S. Here is a list for remider of what I want for christmas. If you want you can write back.

Dear Santa
I bin good this
year. I got good
grades in school.
Last year I got
to take one of
your elfs home
her name was
Molly.   Sincerely.
           Jess

4

Odds
and Ends

nyone who is a parent or guardian, or has simply spent time around young children knows the concept of odds and ends—the idea that there are lots of things that just don't fit anywhere else. These may include letters to the reindeer or to Mrs. Claus, unusual questions, requests or gifts, or probes into life at the North Pole and even into Santa's personal life: "How did you and Mrs. Claus meet?" "Do you have any children? And if so, do they get presents from you?" "Why do you have that hair on your face?" They also include statements of opinion: "You're much too old." This is the section for everything that didn't fit somewhere else but we simply had to share it with you.

"How many houses do you have at the North Pole for the elves?"

"Do you go to church on Sundays?"

"When Is your birthday?"

"I've enclosed a magic trick you can master in minutes!"

"I would like a picture of you and Mrs. Claws."

"If your out all nite when do you open gifts?"

"How many kids were bad and how many were good?"

"I am nine years old. How old would I be If I was an elf?"

"What is your wifs first name? What are your elfs names?"

Dear Santa,

I have a North Pole Direct card and I called you. The card only gave me five minutes so I couldn't tell you what I wanted. I never knew you had a 1800 number.

Love,
Andy

Dear Santa
Hi. How are you? I am sick.
I didn't go to school. I might
have a strep throat.
It is sore. Well. It might
be sore. But. The doter will
find out if it is sore today.
I will leave cookcies and milk
for you and you raindeers.
So. How cold, is it in the
north pole? It very, very,
very, very, very cold there?
Yes, I'sapose. If I didn't
spell some words right
please write them right.

                    Youl pal,
                    Jessica

December 12

Dear Santa,

I hope your reinders don't get a cold for the winter. Make sure you get a Chirsmas to. I hope you neverr die. I want the Batcave for Chirsmas and that's about it because I'm not spoild. I wonder how many elfs you have. I hope Ms Claas is doing find and the elfs. I hope you have warm clothes for the North pole because it's very cold up there. Were earmuffs and glofs and a big double big triple big suit. Eat the milk and cookies to. On the cup it says, Milk For Santa and Cookies to. I know why you are so fat to becaus you eat milk and cookies all the time. Merry Chirsmas.

Love Douglas

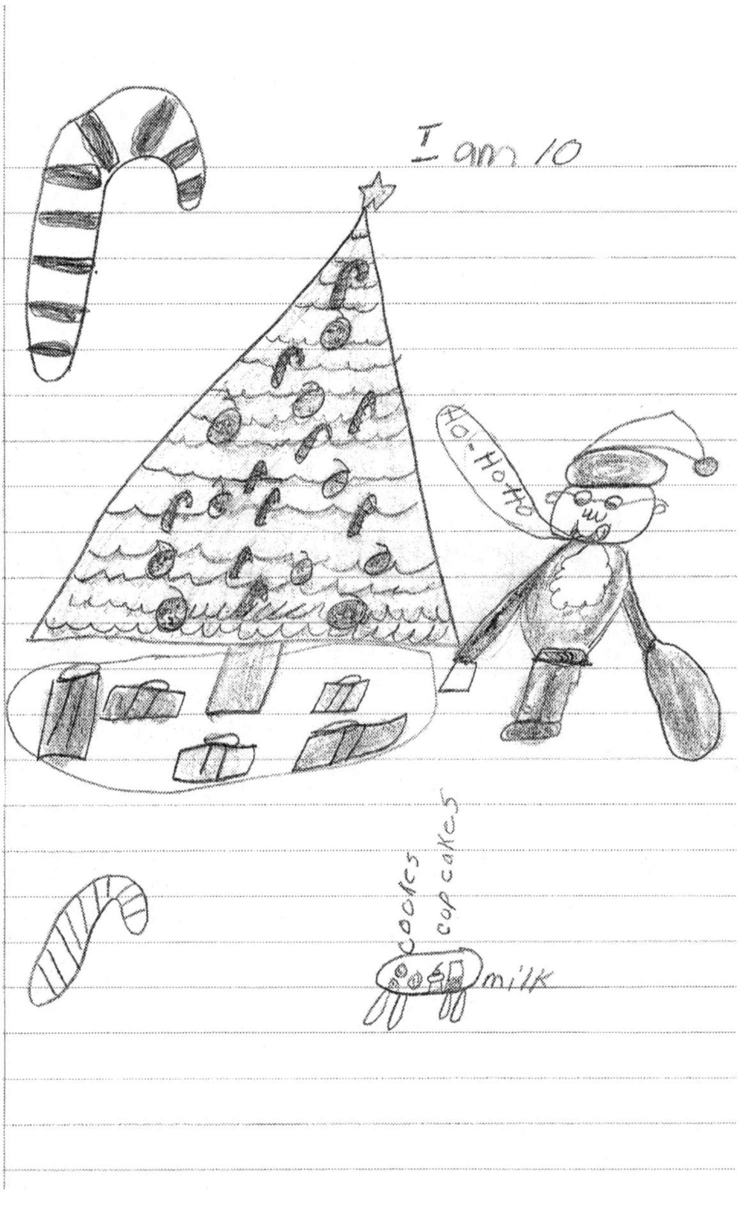
I am 10
Ho-Ho-Ho
cookies
cupcakes
milk

Dear Santa

How many cookies
Can you eat? Do the
reindeer eat cookies?
I will leave you peanut
butter with marshmallow
and milk. If there not
on the table. I probably
ate them. Can I have a
reindeer horseshoe?

singed Brett

Dear Santa

Thank you for George of the Jungle, candys, Pajamas, c.d.. I hope you enjoyd the whisky, beer, prestles. I Love you!

Your doing good!

Love Alexa

Dear Santa,

This year I don't need a whole lot. You see since my brother was in the hospital twice this year, in October and for Thanksgiving, our family hasn't had a lot of time together. I wish you could leave money for the bills or a new car but I don't think you give money or cars. You know about our cars that are both from the 70's and keep braking down and are faling apart. Oh well. Let me just tell you what I would like. The thing I need is a vacation four our family. You know maybe plane tickets or something like that.

List

<u>Vacation</u>
I would realy like to go to Minesota to see my grand parents. (and some snow) If that is too hard maybe you might just send what my family needs righte now.

(brother) He really hs been wanting a SuperNintendo 64. He gets bored a lot now and wants something to do.

(my mom) She wants a car most of all but the other thing she wants is a dishwasher. Ours broke and she doesn't have time anymore to wash the dishes. She is always too tired or busy.

(my dad) he wants a house most of all. But I know there expinsive and hard too find. Actuly I am not sure what he wants. Just send him a thing you think he'd like okay?

I know I am asking for a lot. If I donn't get any of the things I asked for I will understand. Because you usually donn't get me anything. I ges it's because there are more importint things and peple in the world then me. You only have one night anyway. But this year I have been good. I realy tried. I hope you will overlook the time I hit my brother. Last year all did was forget to clean my room and talk bad to momy and you still didn't get me anything. I realy am sorry about yelling at my brother. Honest.

Your realy good girl,
Anne Marie

P.S. I forgot another thing you could do. I would realy like to go to school next year but we don't have enough money. Can you help with that?

Dear Santa,   Dec. 22
   I hope you don't mind me writing on the computer,
because I have a lot to say. First off I want to tell you that
I really do believe in you. And it isn't because I want a lot of
presents, but because I watched a lot of movies about you.
Plus even if you weren't real I would still believe in those
stories about you. As any real kid would do, I have some
questions for you. They have nothing to do with "How come
I can't see you."
   1st Question - How come you are immortal?
   2nd Question - What happens when someone stops
                     believing?
   I really hope you aren't discouraged about those people
who don't believe in you. Because if you do then, you still
have me.
   I'm sorry for making fun of you, but I was around my
friends and I forgot, plus my Dad told me he was Santa
and there was no such things.
   I must go now........um....also I hope you received this
letter in time.

P.S. Here is my Gift List
1. Something nice for mom
2. Something nice for dad
3. Christmas Socks
4. Army Soldiers - Dad already got me them, I found them
5. Spy tools
6. Basket Ball.
7. Necklaces, ring, bracelet

                                             Love,
                                          Stephanie

Dear Santa,

How are you doing? Tell Mrs. Claus hi for me pleas!!! Santa I have been wondering how you make all those toys so quick. I wonder why the toys are name brand. "Oh well!!" Here are the things I want for Christmas . . . a hot set contains ear muffs, gloves and scarf. I also would like an electric blanket. And what ever you bring. Thank you for coming every year and thank you for your time reading this letter.

Love,

Chelsea

Dear Mrs. Claus,

 I am so so happy to finly-finly get to write you a note. I realy-realy-realy wish I could met you in life also the evlse and the raindeer. What I am thinking know is about getting well. It is so boring being sick and at home. I got to go know I have to do my homework.

P.S. It will be a long-long day!!!

Love,

Kala

Dear Santa,

I wonted to come and see you but, I'm sick with the chickin pocks. I do not like them and all so I would allso like my chickin pocks to stop itching and go away. They are diving me crazy I can not stand it any more. I would allso like a new Barbie to. It is colled Sleepover skipper. That is all. Not quite all I would like some surprizes too.

Love,
Sushanna

Dear Santa,

My list for christmas. A sled, sum games for my cenputor, 5 rolls of fim.

Queshen: How can a man got all around the holl vid wourd in one nite?

Gladbeck
Deutschland
01. 12. 1997

Für den lieben Nikolaus haben dieses Bild
Alexander (4,5 Jahre alt) und Theodor (2,5 Jahre alt)
gemalt, mit der Bitte um einen Antwortbrief und gewünschte
Geschenke.

*English translation per Santa's German-speaking elves: For beloved Father
Christmas, this picture has been drawn by Alexander (four-and-one-half
years old) and Theodor (two-and-one-half years old), with the request for
a letter in reply and the requested presents.

Dear Santa,

Santa all I want for Cristmas is a dog and is that so hard to belive because I love dogs. And my step dad sais that we aft to stop bitting my nails we will get a dog but you see I know I need to stop but I also know I really do belive in you if only this once I could get a dog of my very own. And also when it hert Bills feelings about me saying yor not my dad it hurt my feelings to. But you know Santa I really can tell he looks out for me and takes care of me and I really love him.

Love,

Suzanne

Dear Santa,

My name is Nathan and I'm 8 months old. I have been a good boy and even sleep through the night. I eat all my meals and drink all my bottles, so I can grow up smart, caring and strong. I am crawling and trying my hardest to walk. I would like to be able to say mommy for Christmas as this would bring my mommy to tears. Hopefully you will take whatever toy you had for me and give it to another baby who needs it more. Thank you for making all little kids have a great Christmas.

Nathan

To: Rudolph

From: Rachel

Dear Rudolph,
Thank you for leading
Santa's slay. We couden't
have Christmas with out
a bright light like
your's. Now eat a hole
lot and get real strog
for Santa's heavy slay so
all of the little boys/girls
can get there wonderful
presents! Love
              Rachel!

HoHo Merry Christmas

5

P.S.—
Just One
More Thing!

Kids, like most of us, often have some of their best ideas after the fact, and when it comes to letters to Santa they are saved by the good old postscript—the P.S. or the P.P.S. or the P.P.P.S. . . . or even the P.S.S. It seems fitting to close this collection with a selection of treasured, almost left out, last minute inspirations.

 "P.S. Please! Hide my stuff. Note. I'm sorry about the changes."

 "P.S. Santa Claus the stuff on the top of the list I want the most."

"P.S. I think you are a very very good Santa Claus."

"P.S. Wake me up!!"

"P.S. Our house is the one with the skinny chimney."

"P.S.S. I've been good this year."

 "P.S. I feel sorry for you because hardley no one believes in you."

"P.S. I will not be at my house. We will be in North Carolina. Come find me."

"P.S. And bring my mother Bruce Springsteen and Mick Jagger and some warm clothes too." [Note that this postscript had 'strangely mature' handwriting.]

"P.S. Make my parents be a lot nicer to me."

"P.S. The camp I want to go to will be about 200 dollars. In cash."

"P.S. Also please help my brother Neal to walk. Thank you."

"P.S. I love you so so so so so so so so so much."

P.S. Why would people make up Santa Clause anyway if he were not true?

READER/CUSTOMER CARE SURVEY

If you are enjoying this book, please help us serve you better and meet your changing needs by taking a few minutes to complete this survey. Please fold it & drop it in the mail.

Name: _____

Address: _____

_____

Tel. # _____

As a special **"Thank You"** we'll send you exciting news about interesting books and a valuable Gift Cerfificate.
It's Our Pleasure to Serve You!

(1) Gender: 1) ____ Female 2) ____ Male

(2) Age:
1) ____ 18-25 4) ____ 46-55
2) ____ 26-35 5) ____ 56-65
3) ____ 36-45 6) ____ 65+

(3) Marital status:
1) ____ Married 3) ____ Single 5) ____ Widowed
2) ____ Divorced 4) ____ Partner

(4) Is this book:
1) ____ Purchased for self?
2) ____ Purchased for others?
3) ____ Received as gift?

(5) How did you find out about this book?
1) ____ Catalog   2) ____ Store Display
Newspaper
3) ____ Best Seller List
4) ____ Article/Book Review
5) ____ Advertisement
Magazine
6) ____ Feature Article
7) ____ Book Review
8) ____ Advertisement
9) ____ Word of Mouth
A) ____ T.V./Talk Show (Specify) _____
B) ____ Radio/Talk Show (Specify) _____
C) ____ Professional Referral _____
D) ____ Other (Specify) _____

Which Health Communications book are you currently reading? _____

(6) What subject areas do you enjoy reading most? (Rank in order of enjoyment)
1) ____ Women's Issues/ Relationships
2) ____ Business Self Help
3) ____ Soul/Spirituality/ Inspiration
4) ____ Recovery
5) ____ New Age/ Altern. Healing
6) ____ Aging
7) ____ Parenting
8) ____ Diet/Nutrition/ Exercise/Health

(14) What do you look for when choosing a personal growth book?
(Rank in order of importance)
1) ____ Subject   3) ____ Author
2) ____ Title   4) ____ Price
Cover Design   5) ____ In Store Location

(19) When do you buy books?
(Rank in order of importance)
1) ____ Christmas
2) ____ Valentine's Day
3) ____ Birthday
4) ____ Mother's Day
5) ____ Other (Specify _____

(23) Where do you buy your books?
(Rank in order of frequency of purchases)
1) ____ Bookstore
2) ____ Price Club
3) ____ Department Store
4) ____ Supermarket/ Drug Store
5) ____ Health Food Store
6) ____ Gift Store
7) ____ Book Club
8) ____ Mail Order
9) ____ T.V. Shopping
A) ____ Airport

Additional comments you would like to make to help us serve you better.

_____

_____

Thank You !!

‖‖‖

**NO POSTAGE
NECESSARY
IF MAILED
IN THE
UNITED STATES**

BUSINESS REPLY MAIL
FIRST CLASS MAIL PERMIT NO 45 DEERFIELD BEACH, FL

POSTAGE WILL BE PAID BY ADDRESSEE

HEALTH COMMUNICATIONS
3201 SW 15TH STREET
DEERFIELD BEACH, FL 33442-9875

Dear Santa,

The only big thing I want for Christmas this year is the lego hospital. I hope ya have a merry Christmas.

Love,

Kevin is cool

P.S. who puts presents in your stocking at christmas?

Dear Santa,

How are you doing? I'm fine. I'm 19 year old and I don't want nothing for me just for my son. he is one year old and I can't wait for you on Christmas eve I know I am going to get a lot of toys from you I am going to have a big and gigantic christmas trees to put presents under it I also have 3 little brother and sister Please send something for them too.

Sincerelly your
Nancy

P.S. I left some milk and cookies for you. ("low fat milk")

My Christmas List

What I want most of all is for Dad to

stop smoking.

*some surprises

** P.S. The underwear I found in my

stocking last year was not appreciated.

Decmember 25

Dear Santa claus

Hello.
Christmas had just passed, and I didn't recieve a present, Not anything at all. And I am really really sad, because last year I didn't get any thing at all. And my parents gave Just one game for play station. That why I am writing to you. But I Love You

P.S I hope you had a merry Christmas, because I didn't

November 15

Dear Santa,

This might be a little early actuly about 40 days early but this year it might be a little bit more presents than other years but here is my list: oh, wait, from here on I will be writing in green. Okay, now for my list. Teen Niki or Teen Courtney. Tye-Dye Doodle Bear. Sabrina the teenage witch.
Well, thanks hope this didn't take up time oh here's a P.S.

P.S. Number 1- what I am writing you is Plus Santa.

P.S. Number 2 - please Santa I would do anything for a new dad and I don't mind if it's not a new dad but just someone that pays child support!!!!!!

Dear Santa,

I want a paintball gun with

paintballs

P.S.

Please let my dad have a paintball gun

too so he won't get jealous over it.

Thank you

your friend

Brad

Dear Santa,

I was just wondering if I was on the good list or the bad list this year. What are some of the presents I'm going to get this year? _____,

_____, _____,

_____, and a

_____ . How old are you?

_____ . Am I geting any

LEGOs? _____. And I want a video game called Treasures of the Deep.

Love, Max

P.S. Are you real or not?

_____.

If you don't tell the truth that will be a sin you know. So are you real?

_____

Dear Santa

I just want to tell you that
all I want for Christmas is a bed
for me and my 3 year old sister.
I leave with my mom or
dad. My mom can't get me
anything because she has
beening very, veny sick. It is OK
if I don't resive toys but as long
as my sister gets a nice bed.

P.S. I will start beening good

I Love you so, so much

P.S. If you can use your magic, the most thing I want is for my brother to wear clothes that fit him.

Dear Santa,

This Christmas I wouldn't
like but two things. You don't
have to get me bath of
them nor do yo have to
get me eather one of
them but I would like
for you to get me something
please. I would like yo to
get me a magic nuresy
baby and a Calon writer.
(The choclate chip cookies
and hot coca will be
waiting for you Christmas
Eve.)

                    Your friend,
                         Krist

P.S. We don't
    have a chimny
    so you will
    have to find
    another
    way in.

P.S. Can you make a christmas tree that can last one day, then disapeer. My dad gets sick of putting up the tree and taking it down.

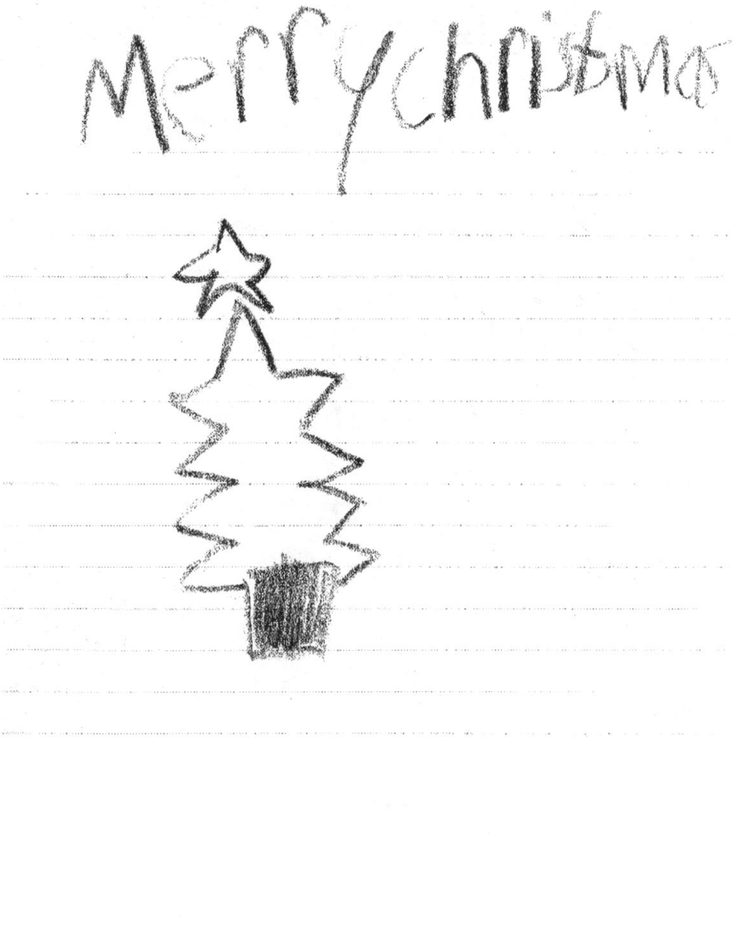
Merry christmas

Dear Santa,

How are ya'? What I really would like is Adidas shoes. Other than that you can surprise me with any thing you think I'd like.

Good luck Christmas Eve:

Love, Krista (11)

P.S.Got a new stocking so dont be fooled!

Dear Santa

this is my list

please surprise me with something

you would think I'd like.

well there is something I would like

two controllers for my sega.

P.S. Don't be scared of my dog.

from

Brandon

I am 8 years old

P.S. My Great grandma is coming down for her frist time since my grandpa died get her something little to make her fill better.

"Merry Christmas"

"I love You"

from: Brianna

Dear Santa ,

Here is some of the things I would like for Christmas. . . . .

whele of frothurn

Monoply

Ms. Pack man

Daytona USA 500

CD things

CD Holder

Crafts

Sand art, Rose art candel makeing thing

fanticte san supprise refills

rose art potery wheel

P.S. I know I am on the "nice" list I got on the internet at www.claus.com

Love
Mallory

Dear Santa Claus,

How are you? I am fine. How are your elves and Mrs. Claus? Guess what, I have been very good this year, I want to know if I could have this radio. It is called Dance Studio. It is so neat. Oh, I really really want some Ty beanie babies. Especially Bones the dog, If your elves can't make him, that is OK. Other ones are fine. I also want boxers, No flowers. I don't just want one pair, I want quite a few. In my stocking I want earings, candy, and ... well, just small stuff like jewelry. I want DEAN Carter CD or tape also, I love Dean Carter, She is so cool, I like her singing. Did you like the cookies Mommy set out for you last Chrismas? I hope you did. Is there an elf named Nikki? You know what? This is how you can find my house. I have different colored lights up, wreths on some windows, My adress is _____ _____ I have white lights wrapped around my tree trunk There are a whole bunch of leaves in my front yard, and I'm the first house on the left of my street,

Turn over Page

I (love) you. Mrs. Claus too. Oh, your elves also. Am I on your Good children List? I hope. I try to be good. Please don't give me a stocking full of coal. I have tried to be coal. I'm trying so hard to stop biting my nails. It is hard. I try though. Oh, guess what!? I am ten. Yup. Not nine anymore. I want a caramell candy called Milk Maid in my stocking. They are yummy. Have you ever tried them? Try one from my stocking if you have not. Your welcome. like my print got I traced my hand. I well, I have to GO! I don't want to, but Alright? to. See ya! Great. Yours Only, Bye. Nikki

Ps. I'm growing my bangs out. PSS. Are you friends with the Easter Bunny?

Dear Santa,

For Christmas I would like another Rings, (My dog.) And a Merry Christmas. And lots surprises.

Love, Katherine

P.S. Have a Merry Christmas!

P.P.S. We love you

P.P.P.S. Could it be the same age as Rings? (9 months old)

P.P.P.P.S. Could it have the same temper as Rings? (Pretty wild)

P.P.P.P.P.S. Could it be the very same as Rings (a good dog but mischfis)

P.P.P.P.P.P.S. Could it be a male?)

Love, Katherine

Dear Santa,

I want a bike, 5 packs of star wars cards, a robe and two TOX cars.

Sincerely,

your friend

tyler.

P.S. My parents say I have enough toys but they agreed these were okay.

Dear Santa

For cHristmas
I would Like

cLotheS, FrenCH
Fry maker, and
An Ice cream
maker.

P.S. I would
also Like to
See my Baby
Sister, Jackie,
in Kentucky.

Dear Santa Clause

For Christmas I would like a dirtbike with a moter on it a Tantrom a car a remote controld motersikel

That is all I know you have mor kids to think about

P.S. my Mom said okay about the dirtbike with a moter

from Eathan

Dear Santa,

I have been vary good this year, Mommy and Daddy will tell you that they are proud of me, If you can I wold like...

Python in black

combat force rangers

Amtrack trane set

ps. pledon't forget the batteries

P.P.S. I will be in Boston

Dear Santa

Please get me sum of the falowing toys. Glitirrater 2, fantastic sticer macer 3, scroch-n-war, wild-n-wary panter, buny surpris, balto sand ate. If you hav a new klixs cobra.

P.S. dont mined the miscerrectly speld words.

Love

Allie

P.S. Since we last spoke

I have done a good job

for you. I have learned

to go potty all by myself.

Santa,

put the present on the chouch. Sind us

a noat we wont froget the milk, cookys,

carets, with mars. You get home safuly.

P.S. Don't forget about the poor people!

Take one ting you would give to me and

give it to a poor child!

Rachel

A Closing Note

As some of Santa's letters demonstrate, it is an unfortunate reality that many children grow up deprived of the basic necessities for life, health and happiness. When you ask some children what they want for Christmas they respond, "I just want something to eat."

In America, "the land of plenty," there are more than 15 million children who are hungry or at risk of being hungry each month: That equates to about one in every four children. Larry Jones, president and founder of Feed The Children, says, "It's wrong for any child to go to bed hungry."

To that end, Health Communications, Inc. and Feed The Children are teaming up to help fight our nation's battle against hunger. Health Communications, Inc. will donate $ .20 from each purchased copy of *All I Want for Christmas Is . . .* to Feed The Children. These funds will go toward helping feed our nation's hungry children.

Feed The Children is a domestic-based international, nonprofit organization providing food, clothing, educational supplies, and other basic necessities to those who lack these essentials because of poverty, famine, drought, flood, war or other calamities. More than 80 percent of this assistance is sent to help needy children and their families in the United States.

By purchasing *All I Want for Christmas Is...* you support our efforts to feed our nation's hungry children. We also invite you to become even more involved by sending in a tax-deductible gift to Feed The Children to help ease the suffering of children and families in need.

For every dollar you contribute, you enable Feed The Children to deliver five dollars worth of urgently needed food and other essentials to children and families. Please join us in working together to end hunger by sending your gift today. You may send a check or your credit card information to:

Feed The Children
333 North Meridian Avenue
Oklahoma City, OK 73107
Attention: Janey Hays

For more information about Feed The Children,
call 405-942-0228.

We hope you have enjoyed your time spent with *All I Want for Christmas Is . . .* and have a renewed appreciation for the season and the wonderful and magical ways in which children perceive and interact with Santa, their home life, and the world.

There are plans for future collections, and if you would like to have your child's letter to Santa considered for inclusion, please mail the original letter to:

> Santa Claus
> c/o Carl Anderson and Jim Walker Jr.
> P.O. Box 50522
> Austin, TX 78763-0522

We would also love to hear how you felt about the book; and remember to have a happy holiday season.

P.S. Don't forget the milk and cookies!

May God bless,

Carl Anderson and Jim Walker Jr.

About the Authors

Photo by Stan Kearl, Austin, TX.

Carl Anderson, Ph.D., has been recognized as "... one of the country's premier Santas" by *CBS Evening News*, "the most realistic Santa Claus anywhere" by KABC-TV, and "the world's foremost Santa expert" by *Los Angeles Magazine*. With a remarkable resemblance to Santa, and a warm, sincere and jolly portrayal, he has been featured on the *CBS Evening News*, CNN and NPR. He has been the subject of articles in *People, The Wall Street Journal, Life, USA Today*, the *Los Angeles Times*, numerous other newspapers and magazines and a guest on a wide variety of TV and radio talk shows.

A licensed psychologist, professional storyteller, speaker, entertainer and an adjunct faculty member at the Educational Psychology Department of the University of Texas, Carl lives in Austin, Texas. He has authored, produced, and performed a wide variety of theatrical works for children, families and adults including *Hold On To Your Dreams, Making Friends*, and *The Santa Chronicles*. Each year from Thanksgiving to Christmas Eve, as Santa, Carl tells stories to and visits with thousands of kids-of-all-ages at the prestigious NorthPark Center in Dallas.

Carl's research into children's reactions to Santa for his dissertation earned him the nickname "Santa Scholar." He has also filled fifteen journals with anecdotes and observations of what happens when children visit Santa. Adult audiences delight in these hilarious and touching tales which make up his presentations *Santa Who?* and *A Mascot for Christmas.*

For further information regarding Carl, and/or performance or speaking possibilities, he may be contacted at:

Carl Anderson, Ph.D.

P.O. Box 50522

Austin, TX 78763-0522

Jim Walker Jr. is a professional writer, editor and the author of numerous books, both fiction and nonfiction. He resides in Dallas, Texas, with his wife Kelly and their two Border collies, Jenny and Jackson.

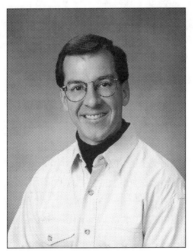

Photo by Hodges Photography, Dallas, TX.

New for Kids

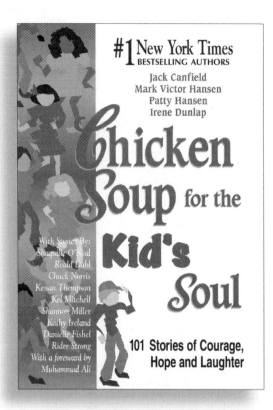

Chicken Soup for the Kid's Soul
101 Stories of Courage, Hope and Laughter
Jack Canfield, Mark Victor Hansen,
Patty Hansen and Irene Dunlap

This special volume contains stories of heroic kids who have overcome tremendous challenges in their lives. It also contains stories that are funny or just plain silly so kids will know that life's challenges are balanced with joy. For readers ages 9 to 13.
Code 6099, $12.95

Available in bookstores everywhere or call (800) 441-5569 for Visa or
MasterCard orders. Prices do not include shipping and handling.
Your response Code is BKS.

New for Little Souls

The New Kid and the Cookie Thief
Story adaptation by Lisa McCourt
Illustrated by Mary O'Keefe Young

For a shy girl like Julie, there couldn't be anything worse than the very first day at a brand new school. What if the kids don't like her? What if no one ever talks to her at all? Julie's big sister has some advice—and a plan—that just might help. But will Julie be too scared to even give it a try?

October 1998 Release • Code 5882, hardcover, $14.95

Now in Paperback!

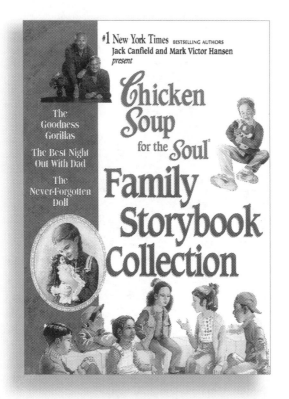

Chicken Soup for the Soul
Family Storybook Collection

The first three little souls are now available in one volume! Inside the covers of this wonderful collection are *The Goodness Gorillas*, *The Best Night Out with Dad* and *The Never-Forgotten Doll*.

Code 6420, 8 1/2 x 11, paperback, $12.95